DICTIO

OF LITERARY

WORDS

VOCABULARY

BUILDING

MANIK JOSHI

Dedication

THIS BOOK IS

DEDICATED

TO THOSE

WHO REALIZE

THE POWER OF ENGLISH

AND WANT TO

LEARN IT

SINCERELY

Copyright Notice

Please note that the content in this book is protected under copyright law. This book is for your personal use only. No part of this book may be reproduced, stored in a retrieval system, or transmitted, in any form or by any means, electronic, mechanical, recording, or otherwise, without the prior written permission of the author.

Copy Right Holder – Manik Joshi
License – Standard Copyright License
Year of Publication – 2014

****

IMPORTANT NOTE

This Book is Part of a Series
SERIES Name: "English Word Power"
[A Twenty-Book Series]
BOOK Number: 07
BOOK Title: "Dictionary of Literary Words"
****

Table of Contents

DICTIONARY OF LITERARY WORDS 1
Dedication 2
Copyright Notice 3
WHAT ARE "LITERARY WORDS"? 6
SECTION - 1 -- Common Literary Words 10
Literary Words -- A 11
Literary Words -- B 13
Literary Words -- C 15
Literary Words -- D 17
Literary Words -- E 19
Literary Words -- F 21
Literary Words -- G 24
Literary Words -- H 25
Literary Words -- I 27
Literary Words -- J and K 29
Literary Words -- L 30
Literary Words -- M 31
Literary Words -- N 34
Literary Words -- O 35
Literary Words -- P 36
Literary Words -- Q 38
Literary Words -- R 39
Literary Words -- S 40
Literary Words -- T 44
Literary Words -- U 46
Literary Words -- V 47
Literary Words -- W 49
Literary Words -- X, Y, Z 51
SECTION - 2 -- Figurative Use of the Words 52
Figurative Use of the Words -- A 53
Figurative Use of the Words -- B 55
Figurative Use of the Words -- C 59
Figurative Use of the Words -- D 63

Manik Joshi 4

Figurative Use of the Words -- E	65
Figurative Use of the Words -- F	66
Figurative Use of the Words -- G	68
Figurative Use of the Words -- H	69
Figurative Use of the Words -- I	71
Figurative Use of the Words -- J and K	72
Figurative Use of the Words -- L	73
Figurative Use of the Words -- M	74
Figurative Use of the Words -- N and O	75
Figurative Use of the Words -- P and Q	76
Figurative Use of the Words -- R	79
Figurative Use of the Words -- S	81
Figurative Use of the Words -- T	84
Figurative Use of the Words -- U to Z	85
SECTION - 3 -- Glossary of Literary Terms	86
Literary Terms -- A	87
Literary Terms -- B	90
Literary Terms -- C	91
Literary Terms -- D	94
Literary Terms -- E	96
Literary Terms -- F	99
Literary Terms -- G, H	101
Literary Terms -- I	103
Literary Terms -- J, K, L	105
Literary Terms -- M	107
Literary Terms -- N	109
Literary Terms -- O	110
Literary Terms -- P and Q	113
Literary Terms -- R	116
Literary Terms -- S	117
Literary Terms -- T	121
Literary Terms -- U to Z	122
About the Author	123
BIBLIOGRAPHY	124

WHAT ARE "LITERARY WORDS"?

'Literary words' are associated with literature.
'Literary words' are typical of a work of literature and imaginative writing.
'Literary words' are used with a particular meaning, in narrative, drama, poetry and other writing in a literary manner.

This book has been divided into three sections:
Section 01: Common Literary Words
Section 02: Figurative Use of the Words
Section 03: Glossary of Literary Terms

IMPORTANT NOTES

NOTE -- A:
ELEVATED WORDS
Use of an 'Elevated' Word in Place of a 'Simple' Word
'Elevated language' is widely used in literature.
Elevated Word -- a word that is used to show a high intellectual level
Simple Word -- a word that is used to keep conversation simple in daily life

Example 1:
'Behold' [elevated word] | 'See' [simple word]
Meaning of 'behold' and 'see':
to become aware of something by using your eyes

Example 2:
'Blithe' [elevated word] | 'Happy' [simple word]
Meaning of 'blithe' and 'happy':
showing or feeling pleasure

Example 3:
'Dulcify' [elevated word] | 'Sweeten' [simple word]
Meaning of 'dulcify' and 'sweeten':
to make or become sweet in taste

Example 4:
'Noontide' [elevated word] | 'Noon' [simple word]
Meaning of 'Noontide' and 'noon':
mid day

******

NOTE -- B:
FIGURATIVE USE OF THE WORDS
Many words and phrases are used in a different (literary) way from their usual (literal) meanings to produce a special effect. *[I have put these words together in **Section-2 (figurative use of the words)** of this book.]*

Example-1:
ache: *In general sense* -- to feel a continuous pain
His leg *ached* because of injury.
ache: *In literary sense* -- *to be very sad*
His false accusations made our heart **ache**. [= made us sad]

Example-2:
Flash: In general sense -- to shine brightly for a few moments
Camera *flashed* once.
Flash: In literary sense -- to suddenly show a strong emotion
Their eyes *flashed* with horror.

Example-3:
Soil: *In general sense* -- the top layer of the earth
The *soil* was very fertile in the plains.
Soil: *In literary sense* -- an area of land; a particular country
These people are very fond of American *soil.*

Example-4:
Thunder: *In general sense* -- (of thundercloud) to make a very loud deep sound
Clouds *thundered*.

Thunder: *In literary sense* -- to cry, shout, complain, or criticize, etc. very noisily and irritably
People *thundered* against the price hike.

'FIGURATIVE LANGUAGE'

'Figurative language' is a form of writing which appeals to the senses. It is a set of literary devices which includes words and phrases used in a different (literary) way from their proper or usual (literal) meanings to produce a special or heightened effect. Figurative language can be classified into different categories based on resemblance, relationship, emphasis, understatement, etc.

******

NOTE -- C:
'LITERARY TERMS'

There are many words which are used to describe particular form of writing in a literary work, or used in analysis, discussion, classification, and criticism of a literary work. *[I have defined these terms in **Section-3 (glossary of literary terms)** of this book.]*

Examples:

catharsis -- the process of releasing strong feelings through artistic activities
diction -- the choice and use of words to create a specific effect in a literary work
epithet -- a word or expression used to attribute special quality to somebody/something
genre -- a particular category, style or type to which a literary wok belongs
holograph -- handwritten piece of writing by its author
idyll -- a poem that describes a peaceful and happy scene
juvenilia -- a literary work produced by an artist, in his/her youth
melodrama -- a literary work that is full of exciting and exaggerated events or emotions
opera -- a dramatic work where a majority of the words are sung to music
panegyric -- a speech or written composition that praises somebody/something

prosody -- the patterns of rhythms and sounds in poetry

quatrain -- a verse of a poem that has four lines

refrain -- a line or number of lines of a song or poem that is repeated after each verse

scene -- one of the small sections within an act (a major division) of a play

semantic -- relating to the meaning of words and sentences

trilogy -- a set of three books, plays, movies, etc. on the same characters or subject

figure of speech -- an expression in which a word or phrase represents one thing in terms of something dissimilar (non-literal) to create a particular effect in somebody's mind, or in which an emphasis is produced by patterns of sound. *[Some common figures of speech are as follows -- alliteration, anaphora, antistrophe. apostrophe, assonance, consonance, hyperbole, irony, litotes, metaphor, metonymy, periphrasis, personification, simile, synecdoche]*

SECTION - 1 --

Common

Literary

Words

Literary Words -- A

abode [noun] -- the place where you live; home

access [noun] -- an outburst of an emotion

adamantine [adjective] -- extremely strong; impossible to break or smash

adieu [interjection] -- goodbye/farewell

afar [adverb] -- at a distance

affections [noun] -- feelings of love, care, etc.

aflame [adjective] -- burning; in flames | full of dazzling lights | showing pleasure or disgrace

afterglow [noun] -- the light in the sky after sunset | a pleasant feeling that you feel after you have enjoyed a good experience; delight

ageless [adjective] -- never coming to an end or growing old; everlasting

agleam [adjective] -- shining strongly; full of light

aglow [adjective] -- shining with color or pleasure

alabaster [noun] -- white and smooth

alchemy [noun] -- magical power

alight [verb] -- (of a bird) to come down through the air onto the ground

amazon [noun] -- a tall, well-built woman

ambrosia [noun] -- delicious food

apace [adverb] -- quickly

anon [adverb] -- before long

arrant [adjective] -- absolute or complete

argent [adjective] – silver; silvery white

arise [verb] -- to wake up; to get up | (of a tall structure; manmade (tower etc.) or natural (mountain, etc.) to become noticeable progressively as you move towards it

arrayed [adjective] -- dressed in beautiful clothes

asunder [adverb] -- into pieces; not together

athwart [preposition] -- from one side to the other side; corner to corner | not in favor of; against to

atrabilious [adjective] -- very sad; bad-tempered

attired [adjective] -- dressed in a specific way

augury [noun] -- a warning for future

aureole [noun] -- round flat shape of light

aurora [noun] -- the dawn

awestruck [adjective] -- feeling extremely impressed by something

awhile [adverb] -- for a moment or short time

Literary Words -- B

badinage [noun] -- friendly comments and jokes

bagatelle [noun] -- a small and insignificant thing or sum of money

baleful [adjective] -- threatening to do something wicked or harmful

baneful [adjective] -- wicked or causing harm

beauteous [adjective] -- beautiful

bedeck [verb] -- to decorate

bedizen [verb] -- to wear dress that is too brightly colored

befall [verb] -- (of something unpleasant) to happen to somebody

beget [verb] -- to produce a child

beggarly [adjective] -- (of sum of money) very small

bejeweled [adjective] -- decorated with jewels

beseech [verb] -- to urgently and eagerly ask for something

bespatter [verb] -- to fill something with drops of water

bespeak [verb] -- to suggest something

bestrew [verb] -- to scatter

bestride [verb] -- to sit with one leg on each side of something; astride

betake [verb] -- to go somewhere

betide [verb] -- to happen

betoken [verb] -- to be a signal or sign of something

betwixt [adverb or preposition] -- between; middle

bid [verb] -- to command somebody to do something; to order

blithe [adjective] -- delighted; unworried

boon companion [noun] -- a true friend or associate

bosky [adjective] -- covered by trees or bushes

bough [noun] -- a large branch of a tree

bounteous or bountiful [adjective] -- giving openhandedly; abundant
bounty [noun] -- supplied in large quantities

bower [noun] -- an enjoyable place in the shade under trees, etc.

braggadocio [noun] -- unreasonably confident behavior

bridle [verb] -- to show annoyance

brink [noun] -- an edge of land

brooding [adjective] -- depressing, inexplicable or intimidating

brow [noun] -- forehead

brume [noun] -- fog or mist

bucolic [adjective] -- relating to the countryside or country life

Literary Words -- C

cadaverous [adjective] -- (of a person) extremely pale, thin and weak

carouse [verb] -- to pass your time enjoying yourself with other people

cast [verb] -- to forcefully throw somebody/something

cataract [noun] -- steep waterfall

celerity [noun] -- swiftness

celestial [adjective] -- connected with outer space

cerulean [adjective] -- deep blue in color

charge [verb] -- to fill somebody with a strong feeling

chasm [noun] -- a deep crack or opening in the ground

cheer [noun] -- an atmosphere of happiness

clarion [adjective] -- loud and clear

cleave [verb] -- to split something using sharp and heavy object; to attach close to somebody/something

clime [noun] -- a country with a particular kind of climate

cockcrow [noun] -- daytime

comely [adjective] -- (of a woman) very attractive

connubial [adjective] -- connected with husband and wife

coquette [noun] -- flirt

coruscate [verb] -- to flash or sparkle

countenance [noun] -- an expression of somebody's face | a person's face

course [verb] -- (of liquid) to flow swiftly

courtly [adjective] -- extremely polite and full of respect; courteous

crabbed [adjective] -- (of writing) not easy to read

crepuscular [adjective] -- related to the period of the late evening

crone [noun] -- an unattractive elderly woman

crucible [noun] -- a situation in which something is tested strictly, turning out something useful or exciting in the course

custom [noun] -- usual behavior

Literary Words -- D

darkling [adjective] -- relating to the dark or becoming dark

dart [noun] -- an strong emotion that is felt suddenly

dauntless [adjective] -- having or showing great strength of mind; not letting anyone prevent you from doing something; determined

deed [noun] -- a particular good or bad thing that somebody do

the deep [noun] -- the sea or ocean

defile [verb] -- to make something (important or holy) dirty or impure; taint

delicious [adjective] -- extremely pleasant or pleasurable

dell [noun] -- a small valley with trees

demiurge [noun] -- a living creature that is said to have created the world

descry [verb] -- to look at somebody/something suddenly

desolate [verb] -- to be totally hopeless

despoil [verb] -- to forcefully steal things from a place | to destroy or desecrate a place

dingle [noun] -- a deep wooded valley

discomfit [verb] -- to confuse somebody very much

divers [adjective] -- of varying types

dolorous [adjective] -- feeling or showing great unhappiness or discontent

dome [noun] -- a stately building

dominion [noun] -- authoritative power

dregs [noun] -- the last parts of something; remains

draught [noun] -- medicine in a liquid form

dulcify [verb] -- to sweeten

dusky [adjective] -- grayish or shadowy

dwell [verb] -- to stay somewhere for a long time

Literary Words -- E

earthbound [adjective] -- not spiritual | not having much imagination

earthly [adjective] -- connected with physical existence, nothing to do with spirituality

easeful [adjective] -- that can help you to get relief or comfort
easement [noun] -- a state or feeling of comfort or pleasure

effulgent [adjective] -- producing bright light

elan [noun] -- the feeling of delight and liveliness

eldritch [adjective] -- scary and odd

elegiac [adjective] -- expressing grief about the past or people who have died

elixir [noun] -- a magic liquid for making someone live for ever

Elysian [adjective] -- relating to paradise or similar places | a place of great delight

empyrean [noun] -- the sky

enamored [adjective] -- feeling great affection for somebody

enchantment [noun] -- magic through words
enchantress [noun] -- an extremely attractive woman

enfold [verb] -- to put your arms around somebody to show that you like them | to cover somebody/something entirely

enshroud [verb] -- to cover something completely making it unable to be seen

epoch [noun] -- a long period of time in history, having particular characteristics

ere [conjunction and preposition] -- ahead of; prior to; before

espy [verb] -- to suddenly catch sight of somebody/something

essay [verb] -- to make an effort to do something

etch [verb] -- (of feelings) to be clearly shown in your face

the ether [noun] -- the higher part of the sky or heaven

evanescent [adjective] -- vanishing from memory or sight immediately

eve or eventide [noun] -- the time during sunset; evening

evermore [adverb] -- forever; more and more; always

Literary Words -- F

fabled [adjective] -- well-known and talked about a lot by people, but rarely seen

fabulous [adjective] -- connected with fables

fair [adjective] -- attractive and beautiful | (of winds) light and blowing in the right direction

fan [verb] -- to make an emotion or a feeling stronger

fancy [verb] -- to consider, believe, dream or imagine something

far-flung [adjective] -- distant or remote; stretched over a wide area

farewell [noun] -- goodbye

fastness [noun] -- safe and secured place that is difficult to attack or easy to guard

fathers [noun] -- ancestors of a person

felicitous [adjective] -- (of words) appropriate and suitable; yielding a positive result
felicity [noun] -- the state of being well chosen

fell [adjective] -- extremely wicked or aggressive; brutal

fervid [adjective] -- hot or glowing | showing strong feelings

fetter [verb] -- to contain freedom of somebody

fey [adjective] -- (of a person) not acting in a reasonable way; acting abnormally, strangely or mysteriously

fidgety [adjective] -- unable to remain still, feeling bored

finny [adjective] -- relating to fish

the firmament [noun] -- the sky

flaxen [adjective] -- (of hair) pale yellow

fleer [verb] -- to laugh disrespectfully

fleet [adjective] -- able to run very fast

the flesh [noun] -- the human body when considering its physical needs, rather than the spiritual ones
fleshly [adjective] -- connected with bodily needs

flexuous [adjective] -- full of bends and curves

float [verb] -- to walk or move easily and smoothly

footfall [noun] -- the sound of the steps

forebear (forbear) / forefather [noun] -- a person in somebody's family who died long time ago

foretell [verb] -- to predict

forsake [verb] -- to give up somebody/something

forswear [verb] -- to give up something, especially in official manner

foul [adjective] -- detestable; hateful

fount [noun] -- the source or origin of something important

fountainhead [noun] -- a source, cause or origin

freight [verb] -- to fill something with a particular feeling or tone

frolicsome [adjective] -- playing in a lively and happy way

fugitive [adjective] -- not lasting for long time

fulgent [adjective] -- shining brightly
fulguration [noun] -- a flash like lightning

fuliginous [noun] -- dusky; dark

fulminate [verb] -- to explode violently

furbelow [verb] -- to adorn with trimmings

fustian [noun] -- impressive but ineffective language or speech

Literary Words -- G

gallant [adjective] -- showing extreme courage in a very difficult or tricky circumstances

garland [verb] -- to decorate with 'circle of flowers and leaves'

gelid [adjective] -- extremely cold | very unfriendly

ghastly [adjective] -- awfully pale

ghost [verb] -- to move silently

gild [verb] -- to make something appear bright, as if covered with gold
gilded [adjective] -- very rich; belonging to the upper classes

girdle [noun and verb] -- a thing that encircles something else | to encircle something

glade [noun] -- a small open area of grass in a forest

gladness [noun] -- extreme happiness; delight

glister [verb] -- to shine brightly with little flashes of light

gloaming [noun] -- dusk

gory [adjective] -- full of or covered with blood

gossamer [noun] -- very light material that can easily be damaged

greensward [noun] -- a piece of ground covered with grass

grizzled [adjective] -- having grey hair

grove [noun] -- a group of trees

gyre [verb] -- to whirl or spin

Literary Words -- H

halcyon [adjective] -- delightful

happenstance [noun] -- a pleasant coincidence

harbinger [noun] -- an indication that shows that something bad is going to happen in a little while

hark [interjection] -- listen

harridan [noun] -- an ill-mannered woman

hasten [noun] -- to hurry

hearth [noun] -- home and family life

heartsick [adjective] -- extremely unhappy or disappointed

the heavens [noun] -- the sky
heavenward (heavenwards) [adverb] -- towards the sky

helpmate [noun] -- a helpful partner, especially a wife

hereupon [adverb] -- after this; as a direct result of this situation

the high seas [noun] -- the areas of sea that are not under the legal control of any particular country

hirsute [adjective] -- hairy

hoary [adjective] -- (especially of hair) grey or white because a person is old

honeyed [noun] -- (of words, language or expressions) kind but insincere

house of God [noun] -- a religious building

hubris [noun] -- the fact of somebody being too proud and causing harm to himself/herself

hue [noun] -- a particular color or shade

huntress [noun] -- a woman who hunts wild animals

hymeneal [adjective] -- relating to marriage

Literary Words -- I

idyll [noun] -- an enjoyable experience, occasion, place, or period connected with the countryside

ill humor [noun] -- unhealthy mental condition

illusive [adjective] -- unreal

imbrue [verb] -- to stain one's hand or sword with blood

immemorial [adjective] -- existing for very long time and thus cannot be remembered by anybody

immure [verb] -- to put somebody in a prison or similar place from which there is no hope of escape

imperishable [adjective] -- lasting for a long time or forever

implore [verb] -- to worriedly ask somebody for something because it is extremely important for you

incubus [noun] -- a problem that is difficult to deal with

indrawn breath [phrase] -- sudden and swift breath that somebody takes to show shock and surprise

infernal [adjective] -- connected with the situation of great suffering of the mind or body; related to hell

inglorious [adjective] -- deserving or bringing shame; making you feel ashamed; disgraceful

ingrate [adjective] -- ungrateful

inhume [verb] -- to bury

insubstantial [adjective] -- not genuine or solid; not strongly built

inwardness [noun] -- interest in things connected with feelings, etc. rather than in the physical world

ire [noun] -- extreme anger

irk [verb] -- to make somebody angry or unable to relax

irradiate [verb] -- to make something look animated and better-off

isle [noun] -- an island

Literary Words -- J and K

joyous [adjective] -- extremely happy; showing happiness; making somebody feel pleasure

keen [adjective] -- having a fine edge or point; not blunt | extreme cold

kindly [adjective] -- caring; compassionate

kingly [adjective] -- typical of a king; very impressive

kinsmen [noun] -- a relative

knell [noun] -- the sound of a bell

Literary Words -- L

lachrymal [adjective] -- connected with weeping or tears

lambent [adjective] -- softly glowing or flickering

laden [adjective] -- full of something unpleasant

languor [noun] -- the pleasurable state of feeling lazy

lave [verb] -- to wash or wash over

lay [noun] -- (in past) a song that tells a story

lea [noun] -- grass-filled area of ground

leaden [adjective] -- like lead; not bright grey in color

lenity [noun] -- kindness or gentleness

leonine [adjective] -- like a lion

leviathan [noun] -- a thing that is huge and very powerful

lightsome [adjective] -- able to move quickly; nimble

limn [verb] -- to represent in painting or words

limpid [adjective] -- transparent

lissome [adjective] -- (of a person) thin and good-looking

locks [noun] -- somebody's hair

lovelorn [adjective] -- a person whose love was not reciprocated

lucent [adjective] -- shining

Literary Words -- M

madding [adjective] -- behaving in a foolish manner; making you feel annoyed or wild

maelstrom [noun] -- a hard-to-control scary situation that is full of emotions or confusion

mage [noun] -- a magician or learned person

maiden [noun] -- an unmarried young girl or woman

the main [noun] -- the open ocean

malefic [adjective] -- causing harm

malodorous [adjective] -- having an unpleasant or obnoxious smell

mane [noun] -- long hair of somebody

manifold [adjective] -- many and various

mantle [noun | verb] -- the responsibilities of an important person | to cover the surface of something

mariner [noun] -- a person who sails a boat

marmoreal [adjective] -- made of marble or similar thing

matrix [noun] -- network [a set of lines, roads etc. that are connected to each other]

maw [noun] -- something that is like a big opening and may swallow a lot of things

mead [noun] -- a meadow

mean [adjective] -- unclean; having very little money

measureless [adjective] -- that has no limits; immense or vast

melancholic [adjective] -- feeling or expressing inexplicable sadness

member [noun] -- an arm or a leg

mephitic [adjective] -- foul-smelling

mercurial [adjective] -- energetic and swift | unstable

mere [noun] -- a lake or pond

merrymaking [noun] -- happiness and enjoyment with singing, dancing, etc.

mien [noun] -- a person's look, style or manner that shows their mood

might [noun] -- great strength, liveliness or influence
mighty [adjective] -- very great, strong and powerful

mired [adjective] -- trapped in an inescapable situation

miscreant [noun] -- a person who has done something against the law

moan [verb] -- (of the wind) to make a long deep sound

morn [noun] -- the early time of the day; morning
the morrow [noun] -- the next day; after today; tomorrow

mortal [adjective] -- resulting in loss of life or likely to cause loss of life | extremely serious
mortally [adverb] -- causing death | extremely

mount [noun] -- a horse that somebody ride on

multitude [noun] -- a large number of people congregated together in a public place

murmur [verb] -- to make cautious and discreet complaint about something

mustachioed [adjective] -- having a large moustache which curls at the ends

myriad [noun] -- an enormously large number of something

Literary Words -- N

naught [noun] -- nothing

nescient [adjective] -- lacking knowledge; ignorant

the netherworld [noun] -- the place where bad people go after death

nigh [noun] -- near

nightfall [noun] -- the time in the evening when it is getting to be dark

nocuous [adjective] -- noxious, harmful, or poisonous

noisome [adjective] -- foul-smelling

noontide [noun] -- mid day

numberless [adjective] -- countless; very many

nymph [noun] -- a beautiful young woman

Literary Words -- O

oaken [adjective] -- made of oak (a type of tree that produces acorns (small nuts))

odorous [adjective] -- having an unpleasant smell

odyssey [noun] -- long and adventurous journey

opalescent [adjective] -- changing color like an opal (a type of semi-precious stone)

orb [noun] -- a very large object, shaped like a ball (e.g.: the sun)

orient [noun] -- the eastern part of the world

overlay [verb] -- to add a feeling, feature, etc. to something

Literary Words -- P

pacific [adjective] -- liking peace

paean [noun] -- a song of admiration or victory
pageant [noun] -- series of exciting and different kinds of events

paramour [noun] -- lover of somebody

pellucid [adjective] -- clear enough to see through

peregrination [noun] -- a long and slow journey

perfervid [adjective] -- intense and impassioned

perfidious [adjective] -- that cannot be trusted at all
perfidy [noun] -- not being loyal to somebody who trusts you

perfume [verb] -- (of flowers) to give air a pleasant smell

peril [noun] -- serious danger
perilous [adjective] -- dangerous

perish [verb] -- (of living beings) to die in an unexpected and violent way

pestilence [noun] -- any highly infectious disease that spreads rapidly
pestilential [adjective] -- extremely irritating or infuriating

philippic [noun] -- a bitter verbal attack

piteous [adjective] -- deserving sympathy or causing you to feel sympathy

plaint [noun] -- a depressing cry or sound

plangent [adjective] -- (of sounds or images) sounding sad and without hope

plash [noun] -- a splashing sound

plenteous [adjective] -- existing in large quantity

plumb [verb] -- to try to understand mysterious thing | to be successful in understanding mysterious thing

poesy [noun] -- poetry

portal [noun] -- an impressive entrance to a building

portent [noun] -- a sign that something unpleasant is going to happen
portentous [adjective] -- indicating an unpleasant event for future

post-haste [adverb] -- as swiftly as you can

potentate [noun] -- a ruler with an unrestricted power

potion [noun] -- a drink of medicine or poison | a liquid that contains magic powers

presage [verb] -- to be a sign that something unpleasant will occur

profusion [noun] -- plenty of something

protean [adjective] -- able to change rapidly and effortlessly

puckish [adjective] -- taking pleasure in playing tricks and irritating people; ill-behaved

puissance [noun] -- great power, control or influence
puissant [adjective] -- powerful or influential

pulchritude [noun] -- the quality of being pleasing to the senses

purl [verb] -- to flow with a babbling sound

purlieus [noun] -- the area in close proximity to a place

Literary Words -- Q

quaff [verb] -- to drink something hastily

quail [verb] -- to feel frightened; to show that you are extremely afraid

quarter [noun] -- a forgiving attitude toward your enemies, etc.

quest [verb] -- to search for happiness, peace and similar qualities

quicksilver [noun] -- not firm; changing frequently

quietude [noun] -- calm

quietus [noun] -- respectful end to life

Literary Words -- R

raven [adjective] -- (of hair) black and shiny

ravening [adjective] -- (of animals) aggressive and hungry

recreant [adjective] -- not courageous

redolent [adjective] -- smelling strongly

redoubt [noun] -- a secure place or situation for something

refulgent [adjective] -- shining brightly

rend [verb] -- to tear something apart forcefully

repine [verb] -- to be discontented

repose [noun | verb] -- a temporary rest; break | to be kept somewhere

resplendent [adjective] -- brightly colored and impressive

revel [noun] -- noisy festivity, celebration or entertainment

rime [noun] -- extremely cold condition in which the temperature is below freezing point

rover [noun] -- a person who keeps on travelling from one place to another

rubicund [adjective] -- (of a person's face) appearing healthy and red

ruddy [adjective] -- (of color) red

runnel [noun] -- a narrow and small river or canal

Literary Words -- S

sage [adjective] -- good and sensible because of a lot of experience

sans [preposition] -- without

sapient [adjective] -- having great aptitude, knowledge or understanding

saturnine [adjective] -- (of somebody's facial expressions, etc.) appearing serious and frightening

savor [noun] -- a very pleasant taste or smell

scion [noun] -- a young member of a famous or powerful family

scourge [verb] -- to create problem for somebody

scribe [verb] -- to write

scud [verb] -- (of clouds) to move fast across the sky

seamed [adjective] -- full of deep lines

seer [noun] -- a person who claims to be able to predict something

sentinel [noun] -- a soldier whose job is to watch or protect place or people

sepulchral [adjective] -- making you think of demise; sounding unhappy and solemn

sequestered [adjective] -- (of a place) without noise and isolated from people

seraphic [adjective] -- extremely beautiful and pure | extremely happy

serpent [noun] -- a very large snake

serpentine [adjective] -- having a curving and twisting shape like a snake

serried [adjective] -- arranged or standing closely together in rows

shed [verb] -- to cry

shore [noun] -- country by the sea

shroud [noun] -- a thing used to cover something

sibyl [noun] -- a woman who is thought to be able to see the future
sibylline [adjective] -- puzzling and complicated to know or understand

sightless [adjective] -- not able to see, notice or realize something

silken [adjective] -- glossy, smooth and soft like silk | made of silk

silver [verb] -- to make something become shining strongly like silver metal
silvery [adjective] -- (of a voice) having a pleasing melodic sound

sinew [noun] -- resource of strength

sinuous [adjective] -- having many graceful curves

slake [verb] -- to satisfy a desire or thirst

slant [verb] -- to tilt in a particular direction

slay [verb] -- to kill somebody in a fight, battle or war

slough [noun] -- a soft wet area of land

slumber [noun, verb] -- sleep | to sleep

smite [verb] -- to attack

snow-capped [adjective] -- (of mountains) covered with snow on top
snowy [adjective] -- as white as snow

sojourn [noun] -- a transitory stay in a place far away from your residence, etc.

sorrowful [adjective] -- extremely sad

sough [verb] -- (of the wind) to make a gentle and pleasant whistling sound

spectral [adjective] -- related to a ghost

specter [noun] -- a spirit

spleen [noun] -- anger

spume [noun] -- a mass of small air bubbles that forms in sea waves

spy [verb] -- to see, spot or perceive somebody/something

star-crossed [adjective] -- unhappy because of being unfortunate

steadfast [adjective] -- firm and determined

steed [noun] -- a horse to ride on

stentorian [adjective] -- (of voice) loud and powerful; like a thunder

still [verb] -- to make something cool, calm and quiet
stilly [adjective] -- still and quiet

storied [adjective] -- celebrated in stories

storm-tossed [adjective] -- badly affected or spoiled by storms

stout-hearted [adjective] -- very courageous; bold

strand [noun] -- the land along the edge of a sea, river, etc.

strife [noun] -- very strong disagreement between people or groups of people; discord

stuff [noun] -- the most significant part of something

stygian [adjective] -- extremely dark and threatening

succor [noun] -- help to the people who are in trouble

sully [verb] -- to spoil something | to make something unclean

sunder [verb] -- to forcefully break somebody/something apart

supernal [adjective] -- relating to the sky or the heavens

susurration [noun] -- a whispering or rustling sound

swain [noun] -- a young lover or suitor

sward [noun] -- an area of grass

the sword [noun] -- military power; violence

sylvan [adjective] -- connected with trees and woods

Literary Words -- T

tare [noun] -- an unwanted wild plant growing among crops

tarry [verb] -- to stay somewhere without any good reason

tavern [noun] -- a pub

temerarious [adjective] -- rash or reckless

tempest [noun] -- a very strong storm
tempestuous [adjective] -- with very strong winds and heavy rain or snow

threescore [noun] -- sixty

throng [noun] -- a large number of people congregated together in a public place

tidings [noun] -- news; information

timorous [adjective] -- nervous, shy and threatened

toil [noun] -- very hard, unpleasant and tiring work
toilsome [adjective] -- involving hard work
toils [noun] -- trap that you cannot escape from

tracery [noun] -- a beautiful pattern with lines and curves

transfigure [verb] -- to make somebody more beautiful

transports [noun] -- state of very strong feelings

travail [noun] -- an unpleasant situation that has a lot of difficulties, etc.

tremulous [adjective] -- shaking a little because of nervousness

tresses [noun] -- long hair of a woman

tribulation [noun] -- great physical or mental pain

troublous [adjective] -- full of troubles

tryst [noun] -- a private meeting between lovers

Literary Words -- U

ululate [verb] -- to give a long and loud cry because of pain or sadness

unbidden [adjective] -- without being asked, requested, invited, expected, or provoked, etc.

unbowed [adjective] -- not willing to accept defeat

uncommon [adjective] -- extraordinarily or extremely large in amount or degree

unman [verb] -- to deprive of manly qualities

unquiet [adjective] -- worried and unable to still or calm

unseeing [adjective] -- not noticing anything in spite of your eyes are open

unspeakable [adjective] -- that is indescribable, especially because it is very bad

unsullied [adjective] -- not damaged badly by anything; still in the original condition; not spoiled

uplifted [adjective] -- lifted towards a higher place or position

ursine [adjective] -- relating to bears; like a bear

Literary Words -- V

vainglorious [adjective] -- extremely proud of your own skills, success or accomplishment

valiant [adjective] -- able to do something daring without showing fear; determined or brave

valor [noun] -- the ability to do something daring without showing fear in war

vanity [noun] -- the quality of being insignificant when compared with significant things

vanquish [verb] -- to defeat somebody completely in a contest, race, war, etc.
the vanquished [noun] -- people who have been completely defeated in a contest, race, war, etc.

venturesome [adjective] -- bold and daring

verdant [adjective] -- (of plants, fields, etc.) fresh and green

verdure [noun] -- green and thick plants growing in a particular place

vernal [noun] -- connected with the season of spring (season between winter and summer)

vesture [noun] -- clothing

victor [noun] -- the winner of a battle, contest, war, etc.

virago [noun] -- an aggressive woman who tries to tell somebody what to do

visage [noun] -- face of a person

visceral [adjective] -- resulting from strong feelings or emotions

vista [noun] -- a beautiful view of a wide area of the countryside, a city, etc.

void [noun] -- a huge empty space

voluptuous [adjective] -- bodily

voyage [verb] -- to travel in a ship to unknown parts of the world
voyager [noun] -- a person who travels by ship to unknown parts of the world

Literary Words -- W

wanderings [noun] -- journeys from one place to another without any purpose

wastrel [noun] -- a lazy, spendthrift, careless and stupid or silly person

the waves [noun] -- the sea
wavelet [noun] -- a small wave on the surface of water, especially in a lake, river, sea or other water bodies

waxen [adjective] -- Ill/sick and pale

wax [verb] -- to become larger or stronger

wayfarer [noun] -- a person who likes to travel from place to place, usually on foot

weary [adjective] -- making somebody feel bored or exhausted

wedded [adjective] -- united

welkin [noun] -- the sky or heaven

wellspring [noun] -- a never-ending supply or source of a particular quality

woeful [adjective] -- extremely unhappy

wondrous [adjective] -- extraordinary, gorgeous and remarkable; incredible, amazing

wont [adjective] -- accustomed
wonted [adjective] -- usual

wordless [adjective] -- without making any noise or saying any words; quiet

worldly [adjective] -- connected with the physical world rather than with spiritual things

wrathful [adjective] -- extremely angry

wreathe [verb] -- to twist or entwine

Literary Words -- X, Y, Z

yearn [verb] -- to wish for something very much, when it is not likely to happen

yesteryear [noun] -- the past time, when thoughts and beliefs were different

yoke [noun] -- something that prevents somebody from doing what they want | something that makes somebody's life miserable

yon [determiner] -- yonder; that

youngling [noun] -- a young person or animal

zephyr [noun] -- a light, gentle wind

SECTION - 2 --

Figurative

Use of the

Words

Figurative Use of the Words -- A

abyss [noun]
In general sense -- a very deep wide crack or opening in the ground
In literary sense -- extremely worrying situation | a profound difference between people, nations, etc.
Use in figurative language: We should never fall into **abyss of despair.**

ache [verb]
In general sense -- to feel a continuous pain
In literary sense -- *to be very sad*
Use in figurative language: His false accusations made our **heart ache**. [= made us sad]

ambassador [noun]
In general sense -- a high ranking official, who is representative to a foreign country
In literary sense -- a promoter of a particular activity
Use in figurative language: Folk-artists are **ambassadors of art** and culture.

ambush [verb]
In general sense -- to suddenly and unexpectedly attack someone from concealed position
In literary sense -- to be suddenly surrounded by many people, etc.
Use in figurative language: Celebrities are often **ambushed by** their **fans**.

angry [adjective]
In general sense -- having strong feeling of dislike
In literary sense -- (of the sea/sky) dark and stormy; tempestuous
Use in figurative language: A couple rowed 6500 miles in a very **angry sea** from Morocco to NYC.

antenna [noun]
In general sense -- either of a pair of two long, thin sensory parts on the heads of some insects, etc.
In literary sense -- ability to interpret the slight or complicated signs intuitively

Use in figurative language: His business acumen and razor-sharp **political antennae** helped his rise to power.

apart [adverb]
In general sense -- separated by a distance, of space or time
In literary sense -- in disagreement
Use in figurative language: The ruling and opposition parties remained **apart** on the issue of migration.

armada [noun]
In general sense -- a fleet of armed ships
In literary sense -- a group of excited or agitated people
Use in figurative language: An **armada of protestors** took out the rally on National Highway.

armor [noun]
In general sense -- protective covering made of metal; shield
In literary sense -- something that saves you from bad situation
Use in figurative language: His politeness is his **armor**.

ascend [verb]
In general sense -- to rise; to climb up
In literary sense -- to make progress
Use in figurative language: Many people **ascend the peak of success** in very short time.

avalanche [noun]
In general sense -- a mass of snow, ice and rock falling down a mountainside
In literary sense -- a sudden arrival or occurrence of something in excess
Use in figurative language: The government received **avalanche of complaints** on corruption.

ashes [noun]
In general sense -- remains or ruins that are left after something has been completely burnt
In literary sense -- something that no longer exists
Use in figurative language: Many people have seen their **dreams turn to ashes** because of lethargy.

Figurative Use of the Words -- B

balm [noun]
In general sense -- an aromatic ointment used to soothe the wound
In literary sense -- something that has a comforting or soothing effect
Use in figurative language: Are books **balm** for every wound?

bathe [verb]
In general sense -- to wash your body with water
In literary sense -- to cover something with light
Use in figurative language: The morning sun **bathed** the city in golden light.

bathed [adjective]
In general sense -- wet with sweat or tears
In literary sense -- filled with light
Use in figurative language: Tall towers were **bathed in moonlight**.

battering [noun]
In general sense -- a violent attack that happens repeatedly and causes injury or damages to somebody/something
In literary sense -- a very strong criticism, defeat, etc.
Use in figurative language: British markets and the pound **took a battering** following the Brexit vote.

begging bowl [noun]
In general sense -- a bowl held out by a beggar, etc. asking for food or money
In literary sense -- earnest appeal for financial help
Use in figurative language: Sovereignty and security of the country can only be guaranteed by breaking the **begging bowl**.

bell [noun]
In general sense -- a device which makes a ringing sound
In literary sense -- something that attracts your attention
Use in figurative language: The slower pace of job growth sounded **warning bells**.

birth [noun]
In general sense -- the time when a baby or young animal, etc. is born
In literary sense -- beginning of something new
Use in figurative language: An armed uprising in East Pakistan led to civil war, which **gave birth to the country** of Bangladesh in 1971.

belly [noun]
In general sense -- stomach
In literary sense -- the round, bent or curved part of something
Use in figurative language: Transporting animals across continents and oceans in a crowded **belly of a ship** is unnecessary abuse.

black [adjective]
In general sense -- having the color of coal
In literary sense -- wicked, sad, hopeless, immoral, etc.
Use in figurative language -- The government extended the deadline for payment of tax on **black money** disclosed during the one-time compliance window.

black hole [noun]
In general sense -- an area in space that has so intense gravitational force that no matter or even light can escape
In literary sense -- a place of emptiness, hopelessness, etc.
Use in figurative language -- Many people falls into the **black hole of depression**. || Our organization will not disappear into the **black hole of chaos**.

blanket [noun]
In general sense -- a bed covering made of woolen material
In literary sense -- a thick covering of something that hides something else completely || a thing used to maintain secrecy about something else.
Use in figurative language: The mercury dropped to 2.1 degrees Celsius accompanied by a dense **blanket of fog**. || We saw the chopper disappear into a dense **blanket of cloud** || The tight **blanket of secrecy** only made matters worse.

blinding [adjective]
general sense -- too bright to see
In literary sense -- (of pain, feeling, etc.) too intense
Use in figurative language -- All of a sudden, one day I had a **blinding headache**.

bloated [adjective]
In general sense -- swollen with liquid or gas and unpleasantly bigger than normal
In literary sense -- too much in amount or size
Use in figurative language -- Can anyone make a difference in a **bloated organization** of more than 100,000 employees?

blurry [adjective]
In general sense -- without a clear outline
In literary sense -- not clearly stated, defined, etc.
Use in figurative language -- The **blurry laws** were prohibiting people from benefitting from such an amazing technology.

border [noun]
In general sense -- a line that separated two areas, states or countries, etc.
In literary sense -- a point that separates two different situations
Use in figurative language -- They used specific criteria to define the **border** between addictive and non-addictive behaviors.

bowel [noun]
In general sense -- intestine
In literary sense -- the deepest part of something
Use in figurative language -- They are learning how to mine the precious metals inside the **bowels of the earth**.

breathe [verb]
In general sense -- to take in air; to respire
In literary sense -- to say something to somebody in a very low voice
Use in figurative language -- "Come down from the building", he **breathed**.

burn [verb]
In general sense -- to produce flames, glow and heat
In literary sense -- to experience an extremely strong feeling, etc.
Use in figurative language -- *They were **burning with rage**, guilt, grief, loss, and confusion.*
related words:
burning [adjective] -- (of feelings) extremely strong
burning-eyes [adjective] -- (of eyes) staring at you very hard

Figurative Use of the Words -- C

call [noun]
In general sense -- the act of speaking
In literary sense -- a very strong feeling of attraction that a particular place has for you [e.g.: *the call of your birthplace*]

cancer [noun]
In general sense -- a serious disease caused by random division of cells
In literary sense -- an extremely unpleasant or a dangerous thing that spreads very fast
Use in figurative language -- In many countries, **the cancer of corruption** has been spreading for years.

canker [noun]
In general sense -- a type of fungal disease that destroys the bark of trees
In literary sense -- a wicked or harmful influence
Use in figurative language – Something must be done to curb **the canker of terrorism**.

carpet [verb]
In general sense -- to cover the floor with a carpet
In literary sense -- to cover with a thick layer of something
Use in figurative language -- They **carpeted** the playground **with flowers**.

chain [noun]
In general sense -- a series of connected metal rings used for fastening objects
In literary sense -- something that hinders your freedom, etc.
Use in figurative language -- Education is the tool that can break the **chains of poverty**.

chill [verb]
In general sense -- to make somebody very cold
In literary sense -- to frighten or terrorize somebody

Manik Joshi 59

Use in figurative language -- *The wail of an approaching siren **chilled his blood**.*

chop [verb]
In general sense -- to cut something into pieces with a knife or other sharp tool
In literary sense -- to divide into many parts
Use in figurative language -- *His book was **chopped** up into 85 short chapters.*

cleanse [verb]
In general sense -- to clean your skin, wound, etc.
In literary sense -- to be free from sin
Use in figurative language -- *Our spirits are now **cleansed of all guilt** and shame.*

cloak [noun]
In general sense -- a type of long loose sleeveless coat
In literary sense -- a thing that covers or hides somebody/something
Use in figurative language -- *While they understand the need and benefits of NGOs, they find the **cloak of secrecy** surrounding their expenditures problematic.*

clothe [verb]
In general sense -- to dress
In literary sense -- to completely cover something with something else
Use in figurative language -- *A tangle of Christmas lights **clothed the walls**.*

clutter [verb]
In general sense -- to fill a place with too many things in an untidy manner
In literary sense -- to fill your mind with unnecessary thoughts
Use in figurative language -- *You need to know how not to **clutter your head** with any negative thoughts.*

cluttered [adjective]
In general sense -- full of a too many things in an untidy manner
In literary sense -- (of mind) filled with unnecessary thoughts

Use in figurative language -- *A cluttered house is a **cluttered head**.*

cocoon [noun]
In general sense -- a soft covering that envelops or surrounds a person or thing to give protection
In literary sense -- something that gives emotional, financial, etc. support to a person or thing
Use in figurative language -- *The only way for a boy to grow to be a man is through the nourishment of the **warm cocoon of** a family.*

cold storage [noun]
In general sense -- the large store for keeping fresh or frozen food
In literary sense -- postponement of something for later period
Use in figurative language -- *His case seems to have gone into **cold storage** as no next date has been listed.*

companion [noun]
In general sense -- a person or an animal that accompanies you in travel or with whom you spend a lot of time
In literary sense -- a feeling that you feel strongly or an activity, etc. that you spend a lot of time in
Use in figurative language -- *For many of us, anxiety is a constant **companion**.*

contagious [adjective]
In general sense -- (of a disease) likely to spread by people touching each other
In literary sense -- (of a feeling, attitude, etc.) likely to influence others in a rapid manner
Use in figurative language -- *Candidates' **enthusiasm was contagious** making it very difficult to choose a winner.*

crossfire [noun]
In general sense -- the firing of guns from two or more directions at the same time, passing from the same area

In literary sense -- a situation where two or more groups are involved in attacking or arguing with each other
Use in figurative language -- *In tussle between political parties, students **got caught in the crossfire**.*

crossroads [noun]
In general sense -- a place where two roads meet and cross each other; an intersection
In literary sense -- at a point where you need to take crucial decision
Use in figurative language -- *I was at a **career crossroads** when I began to work with him.*

curtain [noun]
In general sense -- a piece of cloth that hangs in front of the stage in the theatre or in front of the door in the house
In literary sense -- the end of something
Use in figurative language: -- *The **curtain has fallen** on the grand finals of the Metropolitan Opera auditions.*

Figurative Use of the Words -- D

darkness [noun]
In general sense -- absence of light
In literary sense -- evil or wicked
Use in figurative language: Terrorist attacks are perpetuated by the **forces of darkness**.

daughter [noun]
In general sense -- a female child of somebody
In literary sense -- a popular woman who belong to a particular place
In literary sense – After her success in the competition, she felt like she was whole country's daughter.

dead [adjective]
In general sense -- not alive
In literary sense -- forgotten
Use in figurative language: I will never be **dead** and buried as an unsuccessful entrepreneur.

the dead [noun]
In general sense -- the state of being dead
In literary sense -- something that is useless or ineffective
Use in figurative language: We will bring your project back from the **dead** and you will once again lead prosperous life.

death [noun]
In general sense -- the end of life; passing away
In literary sense -- destructive power

descend [verb]
In general sense -- to move down
In literary sense -- (of mood, night, etc.) to come suddenly and swiftly

draw¹ [verb]
In general sense -- to make a picture of something, using a chalk, pen or pencil

In literary sense -- to give a particular impression
Use in figurative language: His autobiography **drew a rosy picture** of his leadership.

draw² [verb]
In general sense -- to move in the particular direction
In literary sense -- to be going to happen soon
Use in figurative language: End of his life is **drawing** near.

derail [verb]
In general sense -- (of a train) to accidentally leave the track; to make a train do this
In literary sense -- to obstruct a process by diverting it from its planned course
Use in figurative language -- There are questions over whether the referendum vote could **derail the peace process**.

descent [noun]
In general sense -- an action of coming or going down
In literary sense -- undesirable decline in moral, social, political or other state
Use in figurative language -- His swift **descent** into economic ruin continued.

distant [adjective]
In general sense -- far away in space or time
In literary sense -- far apart in relationship, resemblance, etc.
Use in figurative language -- More than half of jobs are found with the help of a social tie, whether a friend, relative or **distant acquaintance**.

dress rehearsal [noun]
In general sense -- the final practice of a play in the theatre, in such a manner that it seems to be a real performance
In literary sense -- the final practice of any performance, attack, etc. before the real one
Use in figurative language -- Anti-terrorism experts believed the two major attacks were a **dress rehearsal** for more ambitious attacks.

Figurative Use of the Words -- E

embryo [noun]
In general sense -- a young animal or plant which is in the very early stages of development before birth | unborn human baby in early stages of development
In literary sense -- a thing that has huge potential for development, but currently is in very early stages
Use in figurative language -- The **embryo of an industry** is starting to form.

eminence [noun]
In general sense -- fame and respect that somebody get in his/her profession
In literary sense -- an area or a piece of rising ground

end [noun]
In general sense -- last part of something
In literary sense -- death

evergreen [adjective]
In general sense -- relating to a tree or bush that has green leaves throughout the year
In literary sense -- always popular, present, etc.
Use in figurative language -- Many **evergreen actors** are extremely passionate about cinema.

expire [verb]
In general sense -- to cease to be valid
In literary sense -- to pass away; to die

Figurative Use of the Words -- F

fall [verb]
In general sense -- to go down; to drop
In literary sense -- to die while fighting with enemies in a war; to get martyred

false [adjective]
In general sense -- not true, wrong
In literary sense -- deceitful; not loyal [e.g.: a **false friend**]

fiber [noun]
In general sense -- a thread that is the part of body tissues, cotton, etc,
In literary sense -- each and every part of something

firepower [noun]
In general sense -- the number and size of guns, missiles, or other weapons that a military has
In literary sense -- capability, strength, potential, etc.
Use in figurative language -- Small businesses might not have the **financial firepower** to take on a larger company.

fizz [noun | verb]
In general sense -- bubbles | to produce a lot of bubbles and makes a hissing sound
In literary sense -- cheerfulness, excitement, or liveliness | to show cheerfulness, excitement, or liveliness
Use in figurative language -- They came home **fizzing with enthusiasm** about what they had learnt.

flame [noun]
In general sense -- a hot bright body of ignited gas
In literary sense -- an extremely strong feeling or sentiment
Use in figurative language -- a **flame of revenge**, a **flame of anger**, a **flame of love**

flash [verb]

In general sense -- to shine brightly for a few moments
In literary sense -- to suddenly show a strong emotion

flower [verb]
In general sense -- (of plants) to produce flowers; to bloom
In literary sense -- to become confident and successful

follow [verb]
In general sense -- to come or go after or behind somebody/something
In literary sense -- to do the same thing as done by somebody else
Use in figurative language: He will **follow** his mother to be a musician in the future.

fractured [adjective]
In general sense -- (of a bone) broken
In literary sense -- (of an organization, etc.) split and unable to function properly
Use in figurative language -- The general election produced a **fractured verdict** for the parliament.

fruit [noun]
In general sense -- a part of a plant in which seeds develop
In literary sense -- natural things produced by earth or nature

fruitful [adjective]
In general sense -- productive
In literary sense -- (of land) producing much crops; fertile

fusillade [noun]
In general sense -- a series of shots fired or stones, missiles, etc. thrown in quick succession
In literary sense -- a rapid series of questions, demands, etc.
Use in figurative language -- The spokesperson ran into a **fusillade of questions**.

Figurative Use of the Words -- G

generator [noun]
In general sense -- a machine that produces something, in particular
In literary sense -- something that can create, make, or produce something else
Use in figurative language -- Small and medium-sized enterprises are the most powerful **generator of jobs** in the economy.

germinate [verb]
In general sense -- (of the seed) to starts to grow
In literary sense -- to come into existence and develop
Use in figurative language -- Ideas for new devices began to **germinate** in their mind.

glimmer [noun | verb]
In general sense -- weak and unsteady light | to shine weakly with unsteady light
In literary sense -- a weak sign of a particular feeling, emotion, quality, etc. | to show a weak sign of a particular feeling, emotion, quality, etc.
Use in figurative language -- His eyes **glimmered with excitement**.

gloom [noun]
In general sense -- hopelessness
In literary sense -- dark and shady place

grave [noun]
In general sense -- burial place
In literary sense -- death

guard [verb]
In general sense -- to protect somebody/something from danger or attack
In literary sense -- to hide your thoughts, feelings, etc.
Use in figurative language -- Data on production, imports and exports were **closely guarded** in the company.

Figurative Use of the Words -- H

hard [adverb]
In general sense -- forcefully
In literary sense -- badly and enormously
Use in figurative language: Two local museums were hit **hard** by the economy.

harden [verb]
In general sense -- to become stiff | to make something stiff
In literary sense -- to be very severe, insensitive, etc.
Use in figurative language: He decided to **harden** his heart.

head [verb]
In general sense -- to move towards somebody/something
In literary sense -- to seem to having undesirable results
Use in figurative language: Their business efforts are **heading** in the wrong direction.

heavy [adjective]
In general sense -- weighing a lot
In literary sense -- full of something

heart [noun]
In general sense -- an organ in the chest
In literary sense -- the outside part of the chest where your heart is

hail [verb]
In general sense -- to highly praise somebody
In literary sense -- to call to somebody to attract their attention

heave [noun]
In general sense -- an act or lifting, throwing, etc.
In literary sense -- a rising and falling movement

home [noun]

In general sense -- a place in which somebody lives their family; house
In literary sense -- a place to keep something
*Use in figurative language: They are searching for a **home** to keep all their old junk.*

harvest [noun]
In general sense -- the crops, cut and gathered
In literary sense -- the product or result of an action
Use in figurative language -- The President's foreign visit has yielded a rich **harvest of agreements.**

Figurative Use of the Words -- I

illuminate [verb]
In general sense -- to shine light on something
In literary sense -- to make somebody's face, appearance, etc. seem animated

immerse [verb]
In general sense -- to dip somebody/something in a liquid
In literary sense -- to completely involve yourself in a particular activity
Use in figurative language -- Many students **immersed** themselves in studies.

infectious [adjective]
In general sense -- (of a disease) likely to be transmitted from one person to another through the environment
In literary sense -- likely to influence others swiftly
Use in figurative language -- Her **infectious laughter**, vibrant personality and warm spirit will be remembered by so many.

inside [adverb, preposition]
In general sense -- situated on the inner part of somebody/something
In literary sense -- within the 'mind' of a person
Use in figurative language -- The darkness **inside us** is not something to be fearful or ashamed of.

Inside track [noun]
In general sense -- a shorter track of a racecourse
In literary sense -- a position of advantage
Use in figurative language -- Whether or not he has the **inside track** for the job remains to be seen.

Figurative Use of the Words -- J and K

knock [verb]
In general sense -- to break or move something by hitting
In literary sense -- to badly affect something, to damage
Use in figurative language: His deceit has **knocked my faith** on friendship.

kind [adverb]
In general sense -- caring, friendly or generous
In literary sense -- favorable
Use in figurative language: Rainy season was very **kind** to the farmers last year.

kiss [verb]
In general sense -- to touch somebody/something with your lips
In literary sense -- to move or touch something gently

knee-deep [adjective]
In general sense -- up to your knees
In literary sense -- to be intensely involved in something
Use in figurative language -- Stop bothering someone while they are at their desk **knee-deep** in work.

Manik Joshi

Figurative Use of the Words -- L

land [noun]
In general sense -- the solid surface of the earth
In literary sense -- a country or region, when it appeals to the emotions

liquid [adjective]
In general sense -- fluid
In literary sense -- (of sound/voice) clear and flowing

labyrinth [noun]
In general sense -- an irregular network of passages in which it is difficult to find you way
In literary sense -- something that is too complicated to understand
Use in figurative language -- *There is a **labyrinth** of rules that are difficult, costly and ultimately less safe.*

Figurative Use of the Words -- M

massage [verb]
In general sense -- to rub a person's body with the hands
In literary sense -- to make somebody feel better, smarter, confident, etc.
Use in figurative language -- *I never tried to **massage** his ego.*

material [noun]
In general sense -- things that are needed to perform a particular activity
In literary sense -- a person that is suitable for particular activity
Use in figurative language -- *He is **good material** for the account department.*

mire [noun]
In general sense -- an area of deep mud
In literary sense -- difficult or distressing situation
Use in figurative language -- *The whole country **sank into the mire** because of the arrogance of a few national leaders.*

Figurative Use of the Words -- N and O

nameless [adjective]
In general sense -- having no name | anonymous
In literary sense -- beyond description

nectar [noun]
In general sense -- a sugary fluid secreted by flowers, used by bees to make honey | the drink of the gods
In literary sense -- somebody/something that is very effective and useful
Use in figurative language -- Soft water is **nectar** for a thirsty athlete.

no-go area [noun]
In general sense -- an area that is dangerous, impossible, or restricted for people to enter
In literary sense -- something that is not allowed to be discussed, done, used, etc.
Use in figurative language -- Many subjects are **no-go areas** for children.

obscurity [noun]
In general sense -- the state of being not well known
In literary sense -- the state of being without light

overwhelm [verb]
In general sense -- to have too strong emotional effect
In literary sense -- to fill something completely with water

Figurative Use of the Words -- P and Q

page [noun]
In general sense -- piece of paper
In literary sense -- a significant event or time of history
Use in figurative language -- He voiced confidence that today's students will mark a **glorious page** in the modern history of the world.

pall [noun]
In general sense -- a thick dark cloud of dust, smoke, etc.
In literary sense -- a strong feeling that has filled the atmosphere
Use in figurative language -- The dwindling fortunes of crude had cast a **pall** over biggest oil-producing nations.

poised [adjective]
In general sense -- well-balanced or suspended
In literary sense -- (of a situation) to remain to be the same
Use in figurative language -- Hostages stood **poised** between life and death

possess [verb]
In general sense -- to own
In literary sense -- (of a feeling) to completely control somebody
Use in figurative language -- Her work expresses the frustration and fear **possessed** by refugees.

precipice [noun]
In general sense -- a very steep cliff, mountain or rock
In literary sense -- very dangerous situation
Use in figurative language -- Financial markets were perched on the edge of a **precipice** with negative yields in some countries.

presence [noun]
In general sense -- (of a person) the fact or state of being in a particular place or thing
In literary sense -- a spirit present near somebody

Manik Joshi

price tag [noun]
In general sense -- a label on something that is on sale, showing its price
In literary sense -- cost of an organization, performer, etc.
Use in figurative language -- *She has not yet placed a **price tag on** the budget request she plans to submit to state legislators.*

prick [noun]
In general sense -- a slight pain caused by a sharp point
In literary sense -- a particular sudden feeling
Use in figurative language -- *He said he was ashamed of his false statement and retracting from that due to **prick of conscience**.*

prince [noun]
In general sense -- son of a king
In literary sense -- a man who is considered to be expert in a particular field or sphere

print [verb]
In general sense -- to make a mark, design, etc. on a surface by pressing
In literary sense -- to make a permanent image of somebody/something in somebody's mind
Use in figurative language -- *Certain moments from this trip will definitely **print on your memory**.*

proud [adjective]
In general sense -- too pleased with your achievement
In literary sense -- tall, gorgeous and remarkable
related word --
proudly [adverb] -- *In literary sense* -- impressively

proving ground [noun]
In general sense -- a place or an environment for testing a new product such as machine, vehicle or weapon, etc.
In literary sense -- a place where your skills, etc. are judged
Use in figurative language -- *This tournament is a **proving ground** for players.*

quench [verb]

In general sense -- to satisfy your thirst by drinking water, etc. | to extinguish a fire

In literary sense -- to satisfy your feeling

Use in figurative language -- *He has crossed many oceans to* **quench** *his* **thrust for knowledge.**

Figurative Use of the Words -- R

raw material [noun]
In general sense -- the basic material from which a product is made
In literary sense -- something that forms the basis of something else
Use in figurative language -- Many novelists use their childhood as **raw material** for their novels.

retire [verb]
In general sense -- to stop doing your job
In literary sense -- to go to bed in order to sleep

receptacle [noun]
In general sense -- a container that is used to hold something
In literary sense -- any object that contains something

regain [verb]
In general sense -- to get back you ability, etc.
In literary sense -- to return to your place

reign [verb]
In general sense -- to rule as a king or queen
In literary sense -- to be the most significant part of somebody's attitude, feeling, etc.

resonant [adjective]
In general sense -- (of sound) continuing for a long time
In literary sense -- bringing images, memories, etc. into your mind

resound [verb]
In general sense -- (of a sound or voice) to fill a place with sound
In literary sense -- to be much talked about
Use in figurative language -- Her strength and dignity **resounded** around the world.

rude [adjective]

In general sense -- bad-mannered
In literary sense -- very plain and basic

ruin [noun]
In general sense -- the remaining parts of a building after its destruction
In literary sense -- the effects, results, etc. that is seen after something has been badly affected
Use in figurative language -- *The 21-year-old player - sacked by the club - was compelled to contemplate the* **ruins of his career** *before it got started.*

rule [verb]
In general sense -- to have ultimate authority or power over a state, country, a group of people, etc.
In literary sense -- to have very high influence of somebody/something
Use in figurative language -- *Long before the dinosaurs, hefty herbivores* **ruled** *the Earth.*

rumble [noun]
In general sense -- a long deep sound or series of sounds
In literary sense -- a particular type of feeling or emotion
Use in figurative language -- *There have been* **rumbles of disappointment** *and dissatisfaction.*

Figurative Use of the Words -- S

salvo [noun]
In general sense -- a sudden and very forceful aerial attack by bombs; firing of several guns at a time
In literary sense -- a sudden and vigorous act or series of acts
Use in figurative language -- An official has launched a **salvo of accusations** of corruption involving many powerful people

scales [noun]
In general sense -- an instrument for weighing
In literary sense -- something that evaluates the truth, or other qualities
Use in figurative language -- They claimed the **scales of justice** were not evenly balanced.

shade [noun]
In general sense -- darkness
In literary sense -- ghost; spirit

shopworn [adjective]
In general sense -- (of goods) dirty and imperfect because of being in a store for a long time
In literary sense -- old, useless, etc.
Use in figurative language -- He found something outrageous in the **shopworn argument** she made against him.

signpost [noun]
In general sense -- a sign at the roadside that gives information about the direction and distance of places
In literary sense -- clue or guidance to an unclear issue
Uses in figurative language -- His statements are **signposts** to his future plan.

singular [adjective]
In general sense -- extraordinary
In literary sense -- different from what is normal; odd; weird

slice [verb]
In general sense -- to cut something from something larger
In literary sense -- to deduct something
Use in figurative language -- She **sliced** three-seconds **off** their best lap time to finish second last in the field of 20 cars.

smolder [verb]
In general sense -- to burn slowly without a flame
In literary sense -- to show barely suppressed strong feeling or emotion

snare [verb]
In general sense -- to catch an animal in a trap
In literary sense -- to trap and get somebody/something
Use in figurative language -- Your Smartphone might be all you need to **snare** a liar.

soil [noun]
In general sense -- the top layer of the earth
In literary sense -- an area of land; a particular country
In literary sense -- They want citizens to understand that there must not be any war carried out from **German soil.**

son [noun]
In general sense -- a male child of somebody
In literary sense -- a man who is associated with a particular place, region or country, etc.

steel [noun]
In general sense -- a type of hard metal made of a mixture of carbon and iron
In literary sense -- war weapons

storm cloud [noun]
In general sense -- a dark cloud that is seen during bad weather
In literary sense -- something that is hostile, threatening, etc.

Use in figurative language -- The **storm clouds of extreme nationalism** were gathering all over the continent.

sullen [adjective]
In general sense -- bad-tempered and silent
In literary sense -- full of clouds
Use in figurative language -- Raindrops fell unseasonably from a **sullen sky**.

summer [noun]
In general sense -- the season that comes between spring and autumn
In literary sense -- a year of a person's age

sway [noun]
In general sense -- a movement from side to side
In literary sense -- control or rule over somebody/something
Use in figurative language -- He wants to hold the nation **under his sway**.

Figurative Use of the Words -- T

take-off [noun]
In general sense -- the moment at which an aircraft starts to fly
In literary sense -- ready to come into existence
Use in figurative language -- We are optimistic that online grocery delivery in our region is poised for **take-off**.

tendril [noun]
In general sense -- a thin and curling stem of a climbing plant
In literary sense -- a thin curling piece of hair, grass, etc.

thick [noun]
In general sense -- densely covered or filled with something
In literary sense -- to have plentiful of something; to have too much of something
Use in figurative language -- I found the office **thick with tension**.

thud [noun]
In general sense -- to fall with a low or heavy, dull sound
In literary sense -- (of heart) to beat quickly and strongly

thunder [verb]
In general sense -- (of thundercloud) to make a very loud deep sound
In literary sense -- to cry, shout, complain, or criticize etc. very noisily and irritably
Use in figurative language -- Many of the agencies **thundered** against the false allegations.

tongue [noun]
In general sense -- the part in the mouth that has taste buds
In literary sense -- a language
Use in figurative language -- They run a community visitor program to connect older people with younger adults who share the same **tongue**.

Figurative Use of the Words -- U to Z

veil [verb]
In general sense -- (of a woman) to cover her face with a thin fabric
In literary sense -- to partly or completely hide something from something

vision [noun]
In general sense -- the ability to see
In literary sense -- a person of great beauty

vortex [noun]
In general sense -- whirlpool
In literary sense -- an extremely powerful sentiment or situation that is unavoidable

wake [verb]
In general sense -- to stop sleeping
In literary sense -- to make somebody remind something | to make somebody feel a particular emotion again

whisper [noun]
In general sense -- soft and quiet voice
In literary sense -- (of natural objects like leaves, etc.) a soft quiet continuous sound
Use in figurative language -- I remember the **whisper of the wind** as we slid down hillsides

wreath [noun]
In general sense -- a circular arrangement of flowers and leaves
In literary sense -- a circle of cloud, smoke, etc.

SECTION - 3 --

Glossary of

Literary

Terms

Literary Terms -- A

abridged -- a shortened version of an 'original text'

abstract -- not representing somebody/something in a realistic way; but expressing concepts

accent -- the emphasis placed upon a part of a word in pronunciation

acrostic -- a poem or other form of writing in which first letters in each line can be read downwards to form a word or words

act -- one of the main division or section within a play
rising action -- development of complications in a literary work
falling action -- results of the climax of a literary work
actor -- a person who is main character in a performance

allegory -- a form of writing (story, play, picture, etc.) in which each character or event stands for an idea or a quality, such as morality, truth, vice, etc.

alliteration (figurative language) -- repetition of the initial letter or sound at the beginning of words in a sentence
Examples:
Maria **m**ade **m**illions of **m**arshmallow **m**uffins for **m**any **m**ellow **m**essengers.
Peter **P**iper **p**icked a **p**eck of **p**ickled **p**eppers.
Sing a **s**ong of **s**ixpence.
The **g**irl **g**rabbed the **g**olden **g**oose and ran.
The **t**eacher **t**ook **t**he **t**roublemakers' **t**oys.
There is nothing but **d**eath in the **d**esert **d**uring the **d**ay.

allusion (figure of speech) -- a word or phrase that makes a reference to specific person, event, place, etc. in an indirect way
Examples:
*When he fights me, he will fight the third **World War**. [world war -- very tough situation]*
*He is the **Einstein** of our institute. [Einstein -- a very intelligent person]*

Other Examples:
Cassandra -- *used to refer a person whose predictions for misfortune are ignored [from: Princess Cassandra in ancient Greek]*
Frankenstein -- *used to refer a something that may destroy its creator [from: novel Frankenstein by Mary Shelley]*
Goliath -- *used to refer a very large or powerful person or thing [from: Goliath, a giant in the Bible]*
Helen -- *used to refer an extremely beautiful woman [from: Helen of Troy]*
Machiavellian -- *used to refer a very cunning [from: Niccolò Machiavelli, an Italian politician]*
Solomon -- *used to refer a very wise person [from: Solomon, a wise king of Israel]*

ambiguity -- a word, phrase, or statement that can be understood in two or more ways

anachronism -- the misplacing of any person, custom, event, or object in the wrong period of history

anaphora (figure of speech) -- repetition of the same word or phrase at the beginning of successive lines in prose and verse
Example:
My life is my principle. **My life** is my ambition. **My life** is my inspiration.

antagonist -- an important character who opposes the main character (protagonist) in a literary work

anthology -- a collection of work by different writers and published together in a book

antiphon -- a poetical work where two choruses respond to one another in alternate stanzas

antiphrasis -- a word used to express a sense that is directly opposite to its usual meaning, [e.g.: use of 'best' instead of 'worst']

antithesis -- a word or phrase used to make contrast of words or sentiments in the same sentence.
Example:
To err is human, to forgive divine.

aphorism -- a phrase used to say something wise or true

archaism -- an obsolete word or phrase

aside -- a dramatic device in which a character says something to the audience but that is not intended to hear by the other characters on stage

assonance (figure of speech) -- repetition of vowel sounds followed by different consonant sounds. [Or, repetition of consonant sounds followed by different vowel sounds]
Examples:
*The c**at** s**at** on the m**at**.*
*G**o** and m**ow** the lawn.*
*She went h**ere** and th**ere** and everywh**ere**.*

aubade -- a poem or piece of music appropriate to the early morning

autobiography -- a non-fictional account of a person's life written by that person

Literary Terms -- B

ballad -- a song or poem that tells a story in direct or dramatic manner

bestiary -- a collection of moral tales or fables about real or mythical animals, originally written in the Middle Ages

bibliography -- a list of books, etc. about a particular subject; a list of books, etc. by a particular author | the list of books, etc. used by somebody writing an article, etc.
bibliographer -- a student of bibliography

biography -- a non-fictional account of a person's life written by another person

blurb -- a short description of a literary work, written by the author, publisher, producer, etc. with an intention to entice the readers, etc.

bombast -- words which sound impressive but doesn't mean much

burlesque -- a written composition which represents something in a humorous way to make it look ridiculous

Literary Terms -- C

cacophony -- a mixture of harsh and loud unpleasant sounds

cadence -- the rise and fall of the voice in speech

caesura -- a pause in the middle of a line of poetry

canon -- genuine work of a particular writer

canto -- one of the sections of a long poem

catharsis -- the process of releasing strong feelings through artistic activities

character -- a person or an animal in a literary work
characterization -- the manner in which an author makes characters in a literary work seem real

chorus -- a part of a song or poem that is repeated after each verse

chronicle -- a written record of events in order of time | to record events in order of time

classicism -- simple and elegant style of art and literature, based on ancient Greece and Rome

clerihew -- a short comic poem – about a famous person – consisting of two pairs of rhyming lines

cliché -- a word or phrase that has become overly familiar

climax[1] -- the turning point in a literary work
climax[2] -- a series of ideas arranged in the order of increasing importance
Examples:
simple, intelligent, hardworking, strict, awe-inspiring
look, observe, watch, spy

Manik Joshi

talk, discuss, debate, argue
anticlimax -- a series of ideas arranged in the order of decreasing importance
<u>Example:</u>
officer, miner, beggar, traitor, prisoner

coinage -- a recently invented word or phrase

collocation -- words which are usually found together in a language

colloquialism -- a word or phrase that is used in informal speech, but not in formal speech or writing
<u>Examples</u> *of colloquialisms and their meanings in simple English:*
a big gun -- a powerful person
a hush affair -- a secret affair
a raw deal -- a harsh treatment
a smash hit -- very successful
a tidy sum -- a large sum of money
a vulture -- a greedy person
an ape -- a clumsy person
an ugly customer -- a person difficult to deal with
doggy/doggie -- a dog
fishy -- suspicious
hanky -- handkerchief
hanky-panky -- trickery
hubby -- husband
tough luck -- bad luck
tummy -- belly

comedy -- a literary work that is intended to be funny

composition -- a piece of literary work

concordance -- an alphabetical index of all the important words used in a book, etc. that shows where and how often each word is used

conflict -- a situation of struggle between two or more opposing ideas, feelings, etc. in a literary work

connotation -- an idea suggested by a word in addition to its usual meaning

consonance (figure of speech) -- repetition of sounds in quick succession, produced by consonants within a sentence or phrase
Example:
Shelley sells shells by the seashore.

contents -- the different sections contained in a book

convention -- an accepted technique or style in a literary work

corpus -- a collection of written or spoken texts

coterie -- a group of like-minded authors

couplet -- two consecutive lines of poetry that are equal in length

criticism -- careful judgment about the good and bad qualities of a literary work

critique -- to give your opinion to a literary work

Literary Terms -- D

dactyl -- a unit of sound in poetry that consists of one stress syllable followed by two unstressed syllables

deixis -- the use of words or expression whose meaning depends upon the situation in which they are used

demotic -- (of language) used by the common or ordinary people

denotation -- the actual idea referred by a word

denouement -- the end of a literary work when everything is explained

device -- a term used to describe any literary style

diachronic -- relating to the way a language has developed over a span of time

dialect -- the form of a language that is spoken in one particular region, or by one particular social class

dialogue -- conversation between characters in a literary work

diction -- the choice and use of words to create a specific effect in a literary work

didactic -- designed to impart a moral lesson

digression -- unreasonable departure from one topic to another

dimeter -- a line of verse made up of two feet (two stresses)

dirge -- a song expressing mourning in the past at a funeral

dissonance -- a combination of musical notes that are not pleasing together

discourse -- a long and meaningful discussion of a particular subject in speech or writing

doggerel -- badly written poetry

drama -- a performance (play) intended for an audience in a theatre, television, etc.
dramatist -- a person who writes play
dramatis personae -- a list of all the characters in a play
dramatize -- to present a book, etc. as a play

Literary Terms -- E

edition -- the form in which a book is published

elegy -- a poem or song that expresses sadness on demise of somebody

ellipsis -- the deliberate omission of words from a sentence because they are self-explanatory

emendation -- the act of making changes or corrections to a text

encomia -- a prose or verse that highly praises somebody/something

enjambment -- (in a poem) the carrying of sense and grammatical structure beyond the end of one line, stanza, etc. and into the next

epic -- a very long poem expressing greatness of a person, etc.

epigram -- a phrase or short phrase used to expresses a clever or an amusing idea
Example:
The child is father of the man.

epigraph -- a line of writing, short phrase, etc. that introduces a part of a book

epilogue -- a concluding speech, section, etc. of a literary work

episodic -- comprising diverse and separate incidents

epitaph -- words that are written on a tomb

epithet -- a word or expression used to attribute special quality to somebody/something

essay -- a short written composition on a particular subject

euphemism -- an indirect (or a polite) word or phrase used to refer to something disagreeable, embarrassing or unpleasant
<u>Examples</u> of euphemisms and their meanings in simple English:
a gentleman's gentleman -- an attendant
a hair-dresser -- a barber
a lot of transformation of capital -- a lot of expenditure
a meat purveyor -- a butcher
a minatory expression -- a threat
a professor of the tonsorial art -- a barber
adverse climatic conditions -- bad weather
an operative -- a workman
challenged -- disabled
culinary department -- kitchen
downsizing -- laying off a larger number of employees by a company
enhanced interrogation -- torture of somebody by police in the police station
finny denizens of the deep -- fish
golden years -- later period of life
He has fallen asleep. / He breathed is last. / He has gone to the next world. / He was gathered to his forefathers. / He went the way of all flesh. / His soul has left for its heavenly abode. -- He is dead.
He is fond of the fragrant weed. -- He is fond of tobacco.
He is the majesty's guest. -- He is in prison.
I feel an aching void. -- I feel hungry.
lady-dog -- bitch
lord of creation -- man
mortal remains -- dead body
natal day -- birth day
passed away -- died
expecting -- pregnant
a light-fingered person -- a pick-pocket
She has reached the evening of his life. -- She has grown old.
She is not quite exact in his statement. -- She is telling lie.
Silver and gold have I none. -- I have no money.
snowy locks -- grey hair
This is a canine specimen. -- This is a dog.

to be in the family way. -- to be pregnant
tonsorial art -- the art of hair-cutting
underprivileged -- poor

euphony -- a pleasing sound of a word [e.g.: cellar door]

exposition -- the essential background information at the beginning of a literary work

expurgate -- to remove offensive parts of a piece of writing or a speech before printing or reporting it

expressionism -- a style in art, music, and theatre that tried to express people's feelings instead of showing characters, events or objects in a practical way [This style was popular in early 20th century]

extempore -- spoken without any preparation

Literary Terms -- F

fable -- a traditional short story that teaches a moral lesson, using animals as characters

faction -- a literary work that is combination of fact and fiction

fairy tale -- a story for children about magical beings with a moral

fantasy -- any kind of fictional work

farce -- a type of comedy based on absurd, ridiculous or unlikely situations

fiction -- a literary work based on imaginary events, objects, people, or situations

figurative language -- a form of writing which appeals to the senses. It is a set of literary devices which includes words and phrases used in a different (literary) way from their proper or usual (literal) meanings to produce a special or heightened effect.

figure of speech -- an expression in which a word or phrase represents one thing in terms of something dissimilar (non-literal) to create a particular effect in somebody's mind, or in which an emphasis is produced by patterns of sound. *[Some common figures of speech are as follows -- alliteration, anaphora, antistrophe. apostrophe, assonance, consonance, hyperbole, irony, litotes, metaphor, metonymy, periphrasis, personification, simile, synecdoche]*

flashback -- a part of the literary work that takes you to an earlier point in time, especially to make the present clearer

folklore -- the stories and traditions that belong to a particular region or community
folklorist -- a student of folklore
folk song -- an old traditional song of a particular region or community

folk tell -- an old traditional story of a particular region or community that was passed on to people by words

foreshadowing -- a sign of what is to come in a literary work

fustian -- language that sounds impressive but have little meaning

Literary Terms -- G, H

genre -- a particular category, style or type to which a literary wok belongs

gloss -- an explanation of a difficult word or phrase, in a form of added comment or text

gothic novel -- a story of magic, terror and suspense, set in large old house or castles with ghosts

heptameter: a line of poetry that contains seven stressed syllables
hexameter: a line of poetry that contains six stressed syllables

hiatus -- an omission, or a space, in a piece of writing or in a speech || a break in pronunciation between two adjacent vowels

historical novel -- a novel connected with the events of specific period of history

holograph -- handwritten piece of writing by its author

homily -- a long lecture on moral advice

homograph -- a word that has different pronunciation and different meaning but same spelling

homonym -- a word that is spelt like another word (or pronounced like it) but which has a different meaning, for example Key meaning 'set of answer to problems' and Key meaning 'button on computer keyboard'. The state of being a homonym is called **homonymy**.

homophone -- a word that is pronounced like another word but has a different spelling or meaning

hymn -- a song or prayer of praise in honor of God

hyperbole (figure of speech) -- use of words to extremely exaggerate a statement to express strong feelings, usually in a funny or ridiculous way

Examples:
He has authored billions of books on millions of subjects!
He has seen this movie at least ten thousand times!
He will take millions of light years to lace his shoes!
Her backpack weighed a ton!
Her brightly colored dress hurt his eyes!
Her smile was ten miles wide!
His nose is the size of a helicopter!
His reading room is large enough to have its own zip code!
I am so thirsty I can drink every drop of the ocean!
I am so tired that I could sleep for hundreds of thousands of years!
I can move mountains for you!
I found a dollar note in the street; now I can buy all the palaces across the world!
I have told you a million times to finish your homework!
I like mangoes so much that I can eat a whole mango orchard in a minute!
I will die if I have to read one more sentence, I am so tired!
I'll be there in one second.
I'll never reach the end of the race!
My laptop is as old as the hills!
My office is a million miles from my home!
She has been teaching in this college since the Stone Age!
She has long hair -- at least 1,000 feet in length!
She is skinny enough to jump through a keyhole!
She made enough lunch to feed the whole country!
Skyscrapers can touch the moon!
The ball bounced and hit the sky!
The pile of books reached the Jupiter!
We will love you for a billion years!
Will I have to wait for thousands of years for getting water connection!

Literary Terms -- I

iambus -- a unit of sound in poetry that is made up of one short, weak or lightly stressed syllable followed by one long, strong or highly stressed syllable

ictus -- a beat or syllable that is given more stress than others as a part of a rhythm in poetry

idiolect -- the distinctive way that a particular person uses grammar, vocabulary, pronunciation in a language

idiom -- a group of words whose meaning is different from the literal meanings of the component words
Examples:
writ large -- *easy to see, notice or understand*
come into the world -- *to take birth*
wax and wane -- *to keep on increasing and decreasing in significance*
beyond price -- *priceless or extremely important*
the primrose path -- *an easy life that spoils somebody in the end*
the jaws of death, defeat, etc -- *very close to an extremely unpleasant situation*
under the heel of somebody -- *totally influenced or affected by somebody*
somebody's declining years -- *the last years of an old person's life*
a tissue of lies -- *an untrue story*
do your stuff -- *to be very effective*
sally forth/out -- *to leave a place in a determined or enthusiastic way*
the staff of life -- *basic food (bread or similar product)*
many moons ago -- *long time ago*
on either/every hand -- *on both or all sides*
the flower of something -- *the most excellent part of something*
break of day/dawn -- *early morning*
the breath of life to/for somebody -- *a vital part of a somebody's existence*
breathe your last -- *to pass away*

idyll -- a poem that describes a peaceful and happy scene

imagery (figure of speech) -- language that creates a certain picture in the senses of people reading or listening
Examples:
He served us thick and syrupy juice of mixed fruit. [gustatory sense (sense of taste)]
Some members were shouting in the meeting. [auditory sense (sense of hearing)]
The house smelled of burned coal. [olfactory sense (sense of smell)]
It was dark in the cave. [visual sense (sense of seeing)]
He ran his hands on a fur. [tactile sense (sense of touch)]

incantation -- the chanting of special words that have a magical power

inflection -- a change in the form of a word on the basis of its grammatical function | the rise and fall of the voice when you pronounce a word

interlude -- a short period of time between the parts of a literary work

interpolation -- addition to a written composition

intonation -- a change of pitch when you pronounce a word or syllable

irony (figure of speech) -- an expression in which the meaning is the opposite from what is literally said
dramatic irony -- audience or reader knows something a character does not
situational irony -- inconsistency between what is expected and what actually happens
verbal irony -- words used to jokingly say the opposite of what is literally conveyed
Examples (verbal irony) --
Somalia is the most prosperous country in the world!
The butter is as soft as a marble piece!
The name of an elephant in the zoo was 'miniature'.
What a great idea!

Literary Terms -- J, K, L

jingle -- memorable but nonsensical short song or tune, currently used in television advertisements

juvenilia -- a literary work produced by an artist, in his/her youth

juxtaposition -- placing a person, concept, idea, place, theme, etc. together in order to show a contrast or relationship between them

kitsch -- popular but sentimental literary works that have no real artistic value

lacuna -- an omission, or a space, in an idea, a piece of writing or in a speech

lament -- a song or poem that expresses great sadness on demise of somebody, or on end of something

lampoon -- a funny criticism of somebody

legend -- a story with exaggerated or false account of a historical person, passed on from one generation to other by words

leitmotif -- a short and repeated tune in a piece of music || a repeated idea or a phrase in a literary work

lexis -- all the words, phrases, idioms, etc. that form a particular language

literati -- educated and intelligent people involving in literary works
literary criticism -- the debate, discussion, evaluation, interpretation or study of literature

litotes (figure of speech) -- use of a negative statement to emphasize affirmative meaning

Examples:
Learning a new language is not an easy task [= "Learning a new language is a tough task."]
His performance is not bad at all [= "His performance is excellent."]
A million dollars is not a little amount.
America is not an ordinary country.
We cannot disagree with your point of view.
She is not unlike her mother.

lullaby -- a song in the soft and gentle tone, sung to make a baby or child go to sleep

lyrics -- the words of a song

Literary Terms -- M

malapropism -- a mistake of using a word which sounds similar to the other word, but have different meaning

marginalia -- notes written in the margins of a book, etc.

maxim -- a well-known phrase or sentence that expresses an advice or a truth

measure (or bar) -- one of the short sections of equal length in a piece of music

melodrama -- a literary work that is full of exciting and exaggerated events or emotions

memoirs -- an account written by somebody famous, about their life and experiences

metalanguage -- the words and phrases used to describe a particular language

metaphor (figure of speech) -- a word or phrase used to show that the two things have the same qualities. Metaphor is an implied simile.
Examples:
He has a **heart** of **gold**.
Her **hair** is **silk**.
Her **voice** is **velvet**.
His **daughter** is his **sunshine**
Life is a **roller coaster**. || **Life** is a **journey**.
My **books** are my **friends**.
Our **president** is an **encyclopedia** of information.
The **snow** is a **white blanket** over the mountain tops.
Time is **money**.

metathesis -- a change in the order of letters or sounds, placed in a word

meter -- strong and weak stresses in lines of poetry producing the rhythm

metonymy -- a word or phrase used to refer to something by the name of something else that is closely associated with it.
Examples:
The **bench** passed the order [bench = judges]
The **pen** is mightier than the **sword**. [pen = written words; sword = military power]
Let me give you a **hand**. [hand = help]

mime -- a performance in which expressions are made through bodily movement, without using any words

monologue -- a long speech in a literary work spoken by one character when he/she is alone | *dramatic monologue* -- a dramatic story in verse, told by one person

morpheme -- the minimal unit of grammatical meaning that a word can be divided into

motif -- a recurring idea, phrase, etc. in a literary work

muse -- somebody that is the source of inspiration for a poet, painter, writer, or other artist

myth -- a story with real or unreal account from old times, passed on from one generation to other by words

Literary Terms -- N

narration -- the act of telling a story in a movie, novel or play
narrative -- a story or a description of events
narrator -- a person who tells a story in a movie, novel or play

neologism -- a newly introduced word, phrase or expression or a new meaning of a word, phrase or expression

novel -- a very long story with imaginary characters, events and situations
novelette -- a badly written short novel, usually romantic one
novelist -- writer of a novel
novelistic -- typical of a novel
novella -- a short novel

Literary Terms -- O

octet -- a piece of music for eight musicians or singers

ode -- a poem that addresses to a person or thing in a serious manner

onomatopoeia (figure of speech) -- use of a word whose sound is similar to the noise it describes

Examples:
A **dog barked** on seeing a rag-picker.
Drivers **honked** their **horns** as they drove past.
The **birds** are **chirping** in the garden.
We can hear **patter** of **rain** on the roof.
Who is **knocking** at the **door**?

Other Examples:
booming of guns
buzzing of bees
chinking of glass
clanging of arms
clanking of chains
crackling of fire
dinging of a bell
murmuring of bees
rustling of leaves

Boom! Boom! Boom!
Hiss! Hiss! Hiss
Oh! Oh! Oh!
Splash! Splash! Splash!
Tinkle! Tinkle! Tinkle!
Woof! Woof! Woof!
Splat! | Snap! | Pop!

Also note:

Different kinds of sounds of water -- *drip, drizzle, gush, plop, spatter, splash, splatter, sprinkle, etc.*
Different kinds of sounds of wind -- *swish, swoosh, whisper, whistle, whizz, whoosh, etc.*

opera -- a dramatic work where a majority of the words are sung to music

oration -- a formal speech given at a public occasion
oratory -- the art of making powerful and effective public speeches

oxymoron (figure of speech) -- a phrase that comprises two contradictory words
<u>Examples:</u>

action plan	*deliberate mistake*
additional reduction	*disaster relief*
adult children	*dull roar*
almost exactly	*elevated subway*
altogether separate	*extinct life*
assistant principal	*falsely true*
awfully pretty	*far closer*
backdoor front	*farewell reception*
blue blood	*faulty logic*
calm breeze	*final draft*
cheap jewelry	*fish farm*
citizen soldier	*flying boat*
civil war	*foolish wisdom*
climb down	*foreign national*
cold fire	*forgotten memories*
conspicuous absence	*front end*
constant change	*global village*
constructive criticism	*half empty*
crash landing	*hard water*
criminal justice	*holy war*
cruel joke	*horror comics*
deafening silence	*idle work*
defensive attack	*ill health*

income tax
jumbo shrimp
liquid gas
live recording
living dead
living fossil
local celebrity
major general
minor disaster
modern history
negative growth
never again
new tradition
obstructed view
once again
open secret
original copy
permanent change

personal business
practical joke
pretty ugly
random order
reality show
retired worker
safety hazard
same difference
science fiction
seriously funny
sleep walk
sweet sorrow
top floor
tragic comedy
travel stop
uninvited guest
water vapor
young adult

Literary Terms -- P and Q

paean -- a song of praise or victory, usually related to military

paleography -- the study and deciphering of ancient writing systems

palimpsest -- an ancient manuscript, usually on surface, from which some or whole original text has been removed

panegyric -- a speech or written composition that praises somebody or something

parable -- a short, moral or spiritual story

paradox (figure of speech)-- a statement containing self-contradictory ideas that might be true
Example:
This sentence is grammatically incorrect.

parody -- an amusing copy of a piece of acting, music, writing, etc.

pathetic Fallacy -- the act of describing objects and animals as having human feelings

personification (figure of speech) -- the practice of representing inanimate objects, and abstract ideas or qualities, etc. as human beings
Examples:
An **opportunity knocked** on my door.
Clouds over the mountains were **singing** the song.
Experience is the **highway** to success!
His **car jumped** to the finish line.
Metropolitan **cities** never **sleep**.
The **cookies screamed**, "I'm done!" from the oven.
The **fire swallowed** the entire forest.
The **flowers danced** in the gentle breeze.
The good **news traveled** fast through the town.

The **leaves danced** as the wind blew through the forest.
The **moon smiled** down on a winter night.
The old **buildings** are **calling** me.
The **raindrops smiled** as they gently fell to the earth.
The **sand tickled** my toes.
The **sun** was **playing** hide and seek with the clouds.
The **sunflowers nodded** their yellow heads.
The **wind whispered** through dry grass.
Time and tide **waits** for none.
Time flies when you are having a great time.
Trees were **requesting** him not to cut them.

Note -- **Apostrophe** -- a word or phrase used to directly address an inanimate object and abstract ideas or qualities, etc.
Example:
O terrorism! When will your end come?

phonetics -- the study of sounds of speech

play -- a piece of writing that is performed by actors in a theatre, etc.
playwright -- a person who writes plays for the theatre, television, etc.

plot -- the sequence of events in a literary work

point of view -- the perspective from which a literary work is told. [First person point of view ('I') - the narrator is a character in the story | Third person point of view ('he', 'she', 'they') - the narrator is not a character in the story

polemic -- a speech or written composition that puts strong arguments for or against somebody or something

polysemy -- the fact of having two or more meanings

prologue -- an introductory speech, section, etc. of a literary work

prose -- writing that is not written in the form of verse

prosody -- the patterns of rhythms and sounds in poetry

protagonist -- the main character in a literary work, often with a positive role

proverb -- a well-known phrase or sentence that expresses an advice or a truth

pun or paronomasia (figure of speech) -- Use of a word than can covey more than one meaning in amusing or humorous way, or use of words that have different meanings but the same pronunciation
Example:
*A happy life depends on a **liver**. [liver = a person who lives; liver= an organ]*

quatrain -- a verse of a poem that has four lines

quintet -- a piece of music sung by five musicians or singers

quote -- the exact spoken or written words of a person being referred to

Literary Terms -- R

recite -- to say a poem from memory to an audience

refrain -- a line or number of lines of a song or poem that is repeated after each verse

repartee -- quick, clever and amusing response or reply

revue -- a theatrical show involving dances, songs, plays, etc.

rhapsody -- the expression of great enthusiasm in public speech or written composition

rhetoric -- an influential but insincere public speech or written composition
rhetorical question -- a way of asking of a question to put a point more effectively
Example:
Am I your slave?

rhyme -- a short poem in which the last word in the line has the similar or identical sound as the last word in the next one *(e.g.: gain and pain | main and lane)*

rhyme scheme -- pattern of rhyme among lines of poetry [it is denoted using letters (e.g.: ABAB CDCD EE]

roundelay [noun] -- a short, simple song with a refrain

Literary Terms -- S

saga -- a long story about historical heroes, adventures and brave acts

satirize -- to criticize somebody in a funny way

scene -- one of the small sections within an act (a major division) of a play

science fiction -- a literary work based on imagined scientific discoveries of the future, and usually involves extraterritorial life and space travel

screenplay -- the script of a movie along with instructions for acting

script -- the words written for a movie
scriptwriter -- a person who writes the words for a movie

semanteme -- the smallest or elementary unit of meaning
semantic -- relating to the meaning of words and sentences
semantics -- the study of the meanings of words and phrases in a language
sememe -- a unit of meaning carried by a morpheme (the minimal unit of grammatical meaning that a word can be divided into)

semiotics -- the study of signs and symbols with their meaning

septet -- a piece of music for seven musicians or singers

sequel -- a literary work, which continues the narrative of an earlier one

series -- a number of books, movies, etc. connected to each other by character, plot, setting, etc.

setting -- the place and time at which of the action of a literary work takes place

short story -- a short, fictional prose narrative about one particular event

simile (figure of speech) -- a word or phrase that compares two objects of different kinds, usually using the terms 'as' or 'like'

<u>Examples:</u>

Army man fought **like a lion.**
His complexion is **as white as snow.**
Life is **like** a **bridge.**
Our **students** are **like computers.**
Sand looks **like water.**
She ran **like the wind.**
The **sun** is **like** a **furnace** in the sky.

List of common 'AS...AS' Similes--
as attractive **as** a butterfly
as big **as** an elephant
as black **as** coal
as brave **as** a lion
as bright **as** the sun
as busy **as** a bee
as changeable **as** the moon
as clear **as** crystal
as cold **as** ice
as cunning **as** a fox
as dark **as** midnight
as deep **as** well
as free **as** air
as graceful **as** swan
as greedy **as** a wolf
as green **as** grass
as hard **as** stone
as hot **as** a fire
as hungry **as** a wolf
as light **as** a feather
as loud **as** thunder
as proud **as** a peacock
as quick **as** a wink
as red **as** blood

as round **as** a ball
as sharp **as** a razor
as slow **as** a snail
as smooth **as** silk
as soft **as** butter
as soft **as** wax
as sour **as** vinegar
as sure **as** death
as sweet **as** honey
as weak **as** kitten
as white **as** snow
as yellow **as** saffron

soliloquy -- a dramatic device in which a character is alone and speaks his or her thoughts

song -- a lyric poem, with several duplicated stanzas

sonnet -- a poem with 14 lines, and a fixed pattern of rhyme (each line of sonnet contains 10 syllables)

spoof -- a humorous copy of a film/movie, etc. exaggerating its main features

stanza -- a group of lines that form a unit in a poem

stereotype -- fixed, conventional ideas about characters or plots in a literary work

stress -- an extra force applied when pronouncing a particular word or syllable

strophe -- a group of lines that form a section of a poem

style -- the features of a literary work that make it typical of a particular author, artists, etc.

subplot -- a sequence of actions in a drama, novel, etc. that is less or more separate from but related to the main story

subtext -- a hidden meaning in a literary work

symbolism (figure of speech) -- words or expression (denoting something tangible or visible) that are used in place or to represent abstract or universal ideas or emotions
Example:
We were filled with pride at the sight of our National flag.
Objects and symbols they denote:
black color -- evil
bridge -- link between two things
broken mirror -- separation
dove -- peace
green light -- permission
ladder -- connection between the heaven and the earth
red rose -- love
rock -- determination
spring -- youth
stage -- world
the sun -- life
wall -- defense

synchronic -- relating to a language as it is at a given time

synecdoche (figure of speech) -- a word or phrase in which a part of something is used to designate the whole of something or a whole is used to designate the part of something.
Examples:
*She has many **mouths** to feed. [mouths (part) = persons (whole)]*
***India** won by one run in the final. [India (whole) = Indian team (part)]*

syntax -- the way that words and phrases are arranged to form sentences in a language

Literary Terms -- T

tale -- a short story, full of action and adventure

tercet -- a group of three verse lines that rhyme with either each other or with the three lines before or after it

tetralogy -- a group of four books, plays, movies, etc. on the same characters or subject

theme -- the underlying main idea of a literary work

thesis -- long piece of writing by a student for a university degree, based on his/her self-research

tragedy -- a serious and sad play or novel

treatise -- a long and serious written composition to examine a particular subject

trilogy -- a set of three books, plays, movies, etc. on the same characters or subject

tone -- the general character and attitude of a literary work

Literary Terms -- U to Z

vernacular -- the local language spoken in a particular region or by a particular social class

verse -- a unit of a poem or song, comprising of a group of lines
blank verse -- poetry that has a regular rhythm but not rhyme
free verse -- poetry that has neither a regular rhythm nor rhyme

vignette: a short piece of descriptive writing or acting that shows what a particular person, object, situation, etc. is like

wit -- the ability to say or write things that are both clever and funny

zeugma -- a word that refers to two or more other parts of a sentence

****

About the Author

Manik Joshi, the author of this book was born on **Jan 26, 1979** at Ranikhet and is permanent resident of Haldwani, Kumaon zone of India. He is an Internet Marketer by profession. He is interested in domaining (business of buying and selling domain names), web designing (creating websites), and various online jobs (including 'self-publishing'). He is science graduate with ZBC (zoology, botany, and chemistry) subjects. He is also an MBA (with specialization in marketing). He has done three diploma courses in computer too. **ManikJoshi.com** is the personal website of the author.

Amazon Author Page of Manik Joshi:
https://www.amazon.com/author/manikjoshi

Email:
mail@manikjoshi.com

****

BIBLIOGRAPHY

'ENGLISH DAILY USE' TITLES BY MANIK JOSHI

01. How to Start a Sentence
02. English Interrogative Sentences
03. English Imperative Sentences
04. Negative Forms in English
05. Learn English Exclamations
06. English Causative Sentences
07. English Conditional Sentences
08. Creating Long Sentences in English
09. How to Use Numbers in Conversation
10. Making Comparisons in English
11. Examples of English Correlatives
12. Interchange of Active and Passive Voice
13. Repetition of Words
14. Remarks in English Language
15. Using Tenses in English
16. English Grammar- Am, Is, Are, Was, Were
17. English Grammar- Do, Does, Did
18. English Grammar- Have, Has, Had
19. English Grammar- Be and Have
20. English Modal Auxiliary Verbs
21. Direct and Indirect Speech
22. Get- Popular English Verb
23. Ending Sentences with Prepositions
24. Popular Sentences in English
25. Common English Sentences
26. Daily Use English Sentences
27. Speak English Sentences Everyday
28. Popular English Idioms and Phrases
29. Common English Phrases
30. Daily English- Important Notes

ALSO BY MANIK
Simple, Compound, Complex, & Compound-Complex Sentences

'ENGLISH WORD POWER' TITLES BY MANIK JOSHI

01. Dictionary of English Synonyms
02. Dictionary of English Antonyms
03. Homonyms, Homophones and Homographs
04. Dictionary of English Capitonyms
05. Dictionary of Prefixes and Suffixes
06. Dictionary of Combining Forms
07. Dictionary of Literary Words
08. Dictionary of Old-fashioned Words
09. Dictionary of Humorous Words
10. Compound Words in English
11. Dictionary of Informal Words
12. Dictionary of Category Words
13. Dictionary of One-word Substitution
14. Hypernyms and Hyponyms
15. Holonyms and Meronyms
16. Oronym Words in English
17. Dictionary of Root Words
18. Dictionary of English Idioms
19. Dictionary of Phrasal Verbs
20. Dictionary of Difficult Words

ALSO BY MANIK
List of 5000 Advanced English Words

****

Printed in Poland
by Amazon Fulfillment
Poland Sp. z o.o., Wrocław